Untuning the Sky

In Memory of A.J.H.

"Adam, the goodliest man of men"

Milton

"The dead shall live, the living die,
And Music shall untune the sky"
Dryden, "Ode on St. Cecilia's Day"

Untuning the Sky

John F. Hulcoop

PAMINA PUBLISHING
VANCOUVER

Copyright © 2000
John F. Hulcoop

Pamina Publishing
2203 West Fourth Avenue
Vancouver
British Columbia
Canada
V6K 1N9

ISBN 1-894671-00-7

John F. Hulcoop 1930-

Contents

Thriae

Around the boast-rimmed basin
                                        of our Philistian Bay
pebble-dancing
                        leads music-minded feet
to divine
                the sacred location
                                        of alphabet trees:
hermeneutics
                in an olive grove.

Constable's "Stonehenge, Wiltshire"
(for DL)

At the end of this man's rainbow, *hanging*
stones! No peat-bog magic, no miserable
pot of merchant gold, but a vision
of history, before and after: heroism
and suffering. Four hundred men betrayed,
slain here by Hengist in Four-Seventy-Two.
Fell amongst thistles, flints, fits of furze
on the bare, unlovely plain: a landscape
devoid (you might say) of human significance—
apart from Bronze Age barrows humping
like the backs of sleeping giants, warrior-
limbs stirred by the oldest dream of all. See
how they throw the sheet of thin-soiled of turf
that scarcely covers their bones into the air
and let it float back down, sinking into more
centuries of defeated sleep.

                                    If this spot
is magic, the magic must be Merlin's.
Maddened with grief at the death of men,
driven by dreams of a city centered
in music, a civic circle of love,
he commanded the sarsens and big blue
rocks to be clawed out of Africa, and
laid corpse-like on the barren English earth.
Long nights of muttered spells, and doubting days,
he conjured unseen forces and the souls
of men scattering scarlet blossoms
on the dust of hateful death. The seventh day
he slept; waking at midnight, proclaimed
the spells of power and watched as the prone

8

monsters slowly erected themselves
and moved to their proper stations,
turned from isolated monoliths
into trilithons, disposed in bright con-
centric rings, lintels soft with the rainbow's
lucent colours. Thus Merlin refuted
death by breathing life back into memory.

This man turns away from the megalithic
mourning of Carnac, Callanish and Stonehenge,
to cultivate his own backyard, making
it take a human shape, graced here and there
with "monuments of unaging intellect":
mysterious metamorphoses
of money-pots into melodious sights
and coloured sounds: poems, pictures, concerts
and finely printed books.

                    Like Merlin,
he builds his four-gated city, encircled
by service and duty, beauty and love.
New-age alchemist searching for the way,
the magic words that change filthy lucre
into dreams and visions, the foundation stone,
neither mason's nor philosopher's, hangs
in the crystalline air above your head.

Hommage à Paul Delvaux

(pour Ray et Monique)

Behind the eyes
what lies
he finds impossible to say.

A female, *nude et élancé*, reposes
on a pink *chaise longue*, provoking
public opinions.

Prim mouths pursed above crepuscular
jabots, stiff and severe, mutter
discreet condemnations—

but of what
we'd rather not
say.

He might if pressed
but bites his tongue:
il lui est défendu de parler.

Only the brush talks. Every picture tells
une histoire graphique from which those matrons
with their bourgeois bustles and hands,
politely crossed before private parts,
avert their modest eyes.

They also stop their delicate ears
and noses, preferring
not to...

He looks for clues.

The last train to or was it from Mons
or maybe Malines left a little late
or was it a little early? The platforms
stand empty.

Reading between the lines
he sees only sleepers,
concrete ties of disaffection.

A horny feline yowls
nocturnal satisfaction,
her tom, triumphant, sprays
the sage bush, and a distant dog
bays the gibbous moon.

On the Chausée D'Anselmberg
all the shops—their windows on work-days
reflected in the crystallized eyes
of jealous mothers and henna-haired daughters
whose sugared lips moisten
at the mere mention of chocolates
filled with creamy gossip—"are owned
and operated by Jews who know what money means,"
even the shops normally open on Sunday
are shut.

He smells something suspicious
but finds no gefilte fish here.

Five ladies with raised eyebrows frown.
They straighten their whale-boned necks
above black watermarked bows,
smiling to mask malign thoughts.
They appear to acknowledge the pink odalisque
who receives her compassionate pedicure
from the calloused, tender hands
of an out-of-work miner. His home is in Mons
or is it Malines?

The man recording the scene reserves judgement.
They prefer not to...

A ghostly sound, like a train whistle
dying as it disappears into a tunnel,
makes them all look up, even the unemployed
miner.

Green eyes reflect the iron-shuttered shops
and the unpeopled platforms.

This line, he remembers, runs from here
to Berlin, and on into Poland.

Monsieur Poirot ne présent aucune solution finale.

Behind the eyes, white lies,
what lies, he finds impossible...

Wreck Beach
(for WM)

What the human heart hears
in a casual hello
cannot be anticipated
or answered
in a single word.

The late summer sun
may slide in slow motion
toward the sea; trees,
casting longer shadows,
may catch late-comers

cruising the path
between sharp sea-grasses
and logs, where bodies
slick with lust and sun
-tan lotion invite a stay;

but what the indifferent heart
hears in a single word
can never be defined,
not when the passer-by
is taken by surprise,

not when the accent
is foreign, and the heart stops
to listen though the feet
obey the mind
and keep on walking—

13

on past the log-booms
and into the bushes
where slippery boys
camouflage themselves
in Arcadian poses,

disguising their fire-
island purposes
and sun-burned passions
by pretending a different
kind of indifference.

Nobody needs to be told
that Here is not the place
for serious discourse,
and Now is not the time
to practice metaphysics.

But what is revealed
in the alien accent
is a glimpse of the Other,
a moment of future,
a chance second chance.

When the heart construes
the simplest word in ways
not to be constrained
by Webster or the OED,
logic and definitions

go to the wall with all
other kinds of commerce,
the quick exchanges,
the ritualized comings
and nameless goings.

This is not a mutual
rearrangement of rocks
on the beach, behind leaves
bright with the rustle
of flesh against flesh.

What I who kept walking
heard when I returned
to return you your word
and the sun disappeared
was a contract for life.

Mini Intermezzo

Tortoise-shell and cow-
gut, an odd combination

concealing between
unstruck strings sufficient

sounds to scale Olympus
music enough to make

Apollo hand over
the noisy symbols

of power for a liar's
fictional ravishments

Re-enacting Holy Saturday

Benched on hot stone
high in some blasted arena,
sun-curst,kiln-set,fully-fired,
my mind glazes over
an empty vessel loud
with furious sound:
stage for spectacular acts
of frenzied pointlessness
a theater of cruelty.

Dis figuring reality
I sit in a sunny, suburban garden
on a pre-easter morning
sharing this holy blank
with an over-robust red-breast
(too big, by English standards,
to play Christopher Robin), a foul-mouthed
comic blue-jay cracking dirty jokes
in the walnut tree, and bees
buzzing out their honied chorus
like a swarm of dancing doo-doo girls
hummin' round Ray Charles
in the Pepsi-Cola ads.

My untended garden—*things rank and gross
in nature possess it merely*—turns
into another transformation scene
from *Babes in the Wood* or *Puss in Boots*
at the Finsbury Park Empire:
Edwardian tawdry transmogrifying

cross-dressed principal boy-
girls and their male mums
into tits-n-ass floor-shows in Las Vegas—
memories of Minksy's
through layers of nicotine lacquer.

It certainly ain't the set
or cast of characters
anyone expects to encounter
in the darker moments of Artaud's
plague-stricken delirium.

Yet here the plague rages
in my left eye. Herpes Zoster
and his silent troupe mime
feign gestures of ineFFable pain
against the bombazine backdrop
of my suddenly unlettered brain
ripping apart this Tin Pan Pastoral
Saturday with delicate *dents-de-lion* .

Wild lions' den or cat-house in Memphis?
Burning fiery furnace or backyard pottery
with oven? Daniel, Shadrach
and Ananias or Nebuchadnezzar
maddened by bad biblical dreams?

Down through the thickly-scented air
of my fell Easter vision floats a pappus
fine white hairs breeze-blown

18

airborne alongside apple petals
pollens, allergens, antigens, pollutants,
pest-bearing, all of them, like birds and bees,
powerful enough to trigger off
anaphylactic shock, knocking me out
with corybantic histamines,
a melodrama of the failing immune system.

Dat ever-smiling Stevie-Wonder sun
becomes as it hits the meridian a golden glove
on the fast fist of cannibal Tyson
whose rapacious presence I feel
but whose moves I can't anticipate.
Mashing my face, it splits open lips
and breaks not nose but a theatre-gilded heart.

Here, in the garden
with its secret tomb still sealed
like a toilet in a triple-A motel,
I am betrayed (as in the darker moments
of the darkest tragedies)
by all the frenzied pointlessness of being
alone, loved only from afar
by a power preoccupied
with staging his absence here.

No gold-to-airy-thinness-beat
connects me to him in Connecticut
or the unrisen son who plays out
his harrowing part in the deads'
underground parking lot.

19

Rambling, raving, thrashing and falling
in apoplectic distress, howling
like the madwoman of Mostar
searching for her dead child on the banks
of Curlew River, I know the site of ire:

not the bloodied eye-ball, hard as a stone,
but the heart, crazed, imperfectly glazed
cracking with frustration
at the sight and furious sound
of all these non-events,
all this futile brutality
recreated here or in the coliseum
under the eyes of a sun-blistered audience
trapped without holy intermission
in the ruins of a mnemonic *teatrum mundi.*

Salomé

Exhumed, a brain-dead moon transmutes
green grave light into a deadpan no-man's land.

Herod's world watches, waits, sweats, disturbed
by its own demented beliefs and guilty premonitions.

Empty ritual and the royal striptease distract
lunatic minds, unveiling commonplace lust,

deferring the dreaded, long longed-for moment:
music plays, Herodias sucks her passion-fruit, pleasures

of the privileged flesh obscure the *Prinzessin's* livid
face—whiteness blackens through pain to blood.

She drops the seventh scarf; the drain runs red;
the cistern stinks of silence. Crotch-wet, she croons;

Ah! Ich habe deinen Mund geküsst
Jochanaan...

"*Souvenirs de Florence*"
(for DR)

1. In Florence, everywhere, standing ready
    in sun and shadow

    doused in the soft subaqueous light
    of the Academia

    exposed to bursts of ultra-violet rays
    and tourist-bus

    emissions up on the Piazzale
    Michelangelo

    disfigured by rain and pigeon-shit down
    in the Piazza

    della Signoria where vain Italian
    policeman with white

    gloves wait, wondering what you're going to do
    with those huge veined hands

    and the surreptitious slingshot that hangs
    down your youthful back.

2. Before Mike imagined you, tearing
    human flesh from stone,

    transforming "Giant" into giant-killer,
    I singled you out

wanting you, wanting you to set me free,
moving me always

forward toward the act as yet to come—
there where shadow blacks

out a corner of the blue Hockney pool
on which you float

your belly like a lily on the surface
of my dream,

your long fingers leaving dark marks
on the conrete rim

as you turn your head to speak to me,
a dare in your eyes.

3. Lying on my *chaise-longue* I hear Dinu
    Lipatti playing

    Chopin waltzes on the aquamarine
    refractions

    of your pale underwater limbs and long feet
    flashing like fish;

    I catch a whiff of chlorine in the tangle
    of your summer-

23

coloured hair, self-indulgently smiling
at that lost brunette

in love with his own blind, blond reflection,
no longer surprised

you were destined not to free him but slay
his Philistine soul.

Now I must figure him out of his word-
hoard and let him speak.

4. For this degree no language is required
    no prerequisites

    at all. So when you call to register
    even if it's late

    put your slightly scornful lips to the mouth-
    piece and say whatever

    enters your hyacinthine head; babble
    and gurgle like high

    mountain streams juggling stones or cold bath
    water suddenly

    unplugged. Press your ear to darkness, listen
    for stars—Venus

and horny Mars so rarely in conjunction
with Uranus

as those daily primal screams (the horror-
scopes) remind us both.

5. The oracle behind your staring eyes
   curses and decries

   all talk of unrequited love. So let
   your big toe protrude

   through the hole in your old black sock if you must:
   toe-hole with mouth-piece

   lots of trumpets and timpani pomping
   and circumstancing,

   mixing loud majesterial noises
   and rude raspberries.

   Nothing does not have to make sense to any
   one any more so

   I can stop punishing myself because
   I keep repeating

   your name knowing you won't respond, standing
   there preoccupied.

6. I dreamt you rescued me from my enemy,
   touching my face

   gently with your murderous musical
   hands. I felt like him,

   Saul's son, soon to be lamented. Lucky
   for us, the traffic

   cop was off on his siesta. Could we
   be arrested just

   for looking or making music on such
   perverse instruments:

   you harping on me with your marble fingers,
   me blowing trumpet

   volantaries through the hole in your sock
   great processionals

   for state occasions and dissonant love
   songs for each other?

Les Sylphides—Again

Barishnikov in black and white

            (following in Rudi's footsteps
            defector/director)

                            and all those girls

            with little wings

                            beneath their ghostly

            shoulder blades

                            attitudinizing

            in the same moonlight
            the same ruined abbey

                            haunted

by Nijinsky

        Baldina, Karsavina and Pavlova

                            in Paris before the war
                            to end all wars

by Healey-Kay

        Alice Marks and Peggy Hooker

                            in London blacked-out
                            and bombed night after night,
                            bled white in the dangerous
                            moonlight

            more than forty years ago

and still

      en attitude

            en arabesque. . .

                            caught in the headlights
                            not far from Howard Beach

a black youth
run down on the highway
                              by all those whites
                                        is frightened to death
                                        by the colored cost of living
                  already a ghost, lost
                              to the great white way
                                        Barishnikov as break-dancer
meanwhile while a young man
                        at Lincoln's Center

                                        still wearing Benois' black tunic
                        and white blouse

                                        allows the spirits
of Chopin and Fokine
                        and all those girls
                                    to move him
                                        through prelude, nocturne
            mazurka and waltz.

Bal D'Ardent

Dead of an overdose. "Drugs," they say,
but I think "Life." Patrick Bissell,
dancer, beautiful in absolute blue,
despite the costume and clumsy cape.

P. B. as Superman, square-jawed
clean-cut and flying high
whenever he wants.
No need for trick photography
or special effects, simply the muscle-power
of legs and a quick snort of cocaine.

Patrick Bissell, alive, leaping from earth
like fire, absolute energy.

Dead of an overdose, but taking his bow
over and over again, chest still heaving,
face effulgent with sweat and boyish grin
after soaring through the *Sylvia* pas de deux

American dancer, like young Robbins,
Kidd and Fosse, disciplined body
exploding with love
of absolutes.

Winding and rewinding, playing and replaying
the video, I keep recalling him to life
and yet another curtain call.

Handing Van Hammel forward, he steps back
himself according to cavalier custom,
moves forward again to receive the rose
his partner bestows, both blissed out
like city kids in summer, heat crazy,
hopping in and out of an open fire-hydrant,
heads thrown back to catch the full force
of applause that fountains up and soaks them
to the skin as they come before the curtain
for another kind of fix.

Bissell being Bissell. I dance therefore I am.
Living his life *Fast Forward*.

"But too much pressure," the fans protest.
"Unfair," say friends and former partners,
as if the bureaucrats had forced him
like Myrtha and her gang of ruthless wilis
to dance until he dropped. "They killed our boy.
Gotta get drugs out of ballet." (And jazz and sports?)
Pious music, they play now, but no good for dancing.

No good for Patrick Bissell, addicted to life
dead of an overdose.

Civilized Self-Control
(for SE)

Wind-wracked, a murder of killer
crows tears the sky to pieces
outside my study window,
raucous mobster-bullies
in black shiney suits
rampaging through the neighbour-
hood looking for blood.

Shouting and cursing in foreign
tongues because they can't hit
on the roof next door, they raise it
to the ground, screaming obscenites
into the eye of the storm,
staggering through air,
storm-troopers booting each other

aside, a covey of manic witches
competing for air-space
shrieking and howling
feathers blown awry in filthy rags
of rage. Fighting for greater height,
they clear the roof and vanish—
leaving a black hole in my grief.

Why can't I, sitting here at my desk,
responding to all those who sent
flowers and letters
of condolence, why cant I
rise through the hole in the roof,
leap like a rodeo-rider on to the wind,
go screaming mad and blow?

31

Winter Jasmine

(for Adam)

Even before
the October garden gives up
its ghostly roses
and erases michaelmas daisies,

resigning
itself to snow on blue spruce
and the frigid
arabesques of arching black bamboo,

winter jasmine
whispers its too-early arrival,
making me wish
for what shouldn't be far behind—but is.

A deep depression
has settled over the coast—so
says the weather man,
looking one way and pointing another.

I can see
for myself the low cloud-ceiling
and feel sleet-sharp
claws scoring the air at take-off time.

What little
light there is, by eight or nine, congeals
like doom
in an early Ingmar Bergman film.

I dream through
the orange-scented steam muffling my mug,
eyes meandering
out of the window above the kitchen sink—

and there
at the corner of the frost-flecked deck
a mini-miracle
a minor revelation occurs:

small yellow
flowers, six pointed petals, springing
tacitly
to life among the leafless twigs.

Winter jasmine
grown from a cutting I took from the bush
that rambled
round the backdoor of our old house

where you and Zinc
sprawled in the summer sun watching
her second litter
play, pounce and pose, like comic beasts of prey,

romping
through the tangle of mediaeval green
stalking
ancestors in the enchanted forest.

It's blooming
again today—your birthday—November
the Nineteenth;
more than four years later I can't forget

how it bloomed
and blazed in the empty days after
your death,
delivering false messages of spring

even before
winter showed its unbeatable hand:
my single heart
against the ice-black ace of spades.

In a world
so utterly bereft of meaning
yellow itself
might prove to be the only consolation.

Time To Move On
(for NH)

Too many rocks
on too many beaches
too many empty oceans
invisible horizons
days without sun

too many dates
on crossed-off calendars
too many birthdays
deathdays ghostly
celebrations without him

too many take-offs
into mountain weather
pre-dawn departures
destinations uncertain
too many chairs at the table

time to clear out
closets, give away books
Duran-Duran on vinyl
Ken Danby reproductions
a carefully taped goalie stick

pay Mr Dump
to take away bald tires
the old TV that died after he did
things I can't think
what to do with

time to move on
watch his tree grow
feed bright winter birds
in flight through fire and ice
freeing mind

letting it go
wherever it will
by sea, land, through ageless air
untrammeled by years or
the fear of death

Looking Ahead
for SF)

Looking like Oedipus
ahead, longing to find
what he found at Colonus

I see nothing like him
blinded by all the guilt
undesirable desire

and death. I hear my feet
raking, rasping gravel
trying to stamp out voices

that call—my father's
at sunrise and mother's
at night, begging me to come

home and start again—
as if I could rewrite
the whole damned story so far.

What perverse instinct
drives us always back
to quest the place of origin

even though we know
the road will be empty
as soon as we turn round

all trace of what we wish
to know, all sign of those
we love having disappeared

rubbed out by the shuffling
of our swollen feet,
obscured by the awful need

in us to know and not to
know where we came from
who we are and why what happened

happened to those we thought
we couldn't live without?
Meanwhile we must imagine

some common ground, a park
perhaps, trees, nightingales
transposing silence into flight.

Slow Motion Replay

Propped up against a wall of pillows, peering
through milky cataracts at men's diving
in the L.A. Olympics, my ancient mother mutters
"Always so much better the second time.
Stay for a moment and watch." Turning,
her supper-tray still in hand, I see un-
folding like a fresh young fiddlehead
the airborne body of Greg Louganis, pulling
out of a double somersault and disappearing
into the almost undisturbed surface
of the travel-poster pool. "Much more graceful
the second time," she says, glancing
up like a changeling child but not seeing
the smile on my lips in the flickering
light of the cataract-coloured screen.

Little Peter Moonshine Makes Notes
(for CA)

So, what's the score with Felix Mendelssohn's
Lieder ohne Worte?

"Songs Without Words"—how sing them, even say
the title without words?

What's in a name, you ask. More when it comes
to music than naming

flowers: a rose is a rose, but a ballad
ain't a ballade.

Not Chopin, but Bob Hope's signature tune,
"Thanks for the memory."

Mnemosyne, Mother of nine Muses,
memorializes

the past in words and music. Sudden scents,
a little madeleine

can retrieve lost time, book after book loud
with a billion phonemes.

Just noises meaning nothing but themselves:
like woodpeckers pecking,

clocks tick-tocking, water falling, fingers
plucking elastic bands.

School bands and marching bands, Carl Orff and Souza,
oom-pa-pa, oom-pa-pa —

sound is simply what it says. But this noise
maybe baby's first words:

mama , *papa*, *fort* and *da*. They resonate
beyond bisyllables.

And when we start singing songs and hymns,
motets and arias,

what then? Mozart and da Ponte, Rogers
and Hammerstein, Sondheim

words and music springing from one man's head,
poet-composer—what

have we got? Musical poetry or
music that fills the ear

with word-pictures? Keep it pure, snorts Stravinsky.
It refers to nothing

but itself. Oh yeah! What about *Firebird,*
Petrushka, Rite of Spring ?

Bach's divided voices, pure inventions;
thirty variations

41

enabling Count Keyserling to sleep while
Herr Goldberg counted sheep.

Beethoven's great fugue, an experiment
in sound and form. "Abstruse

and intractable," mutters Stravinsky;
but expressive, says X,

of the man's great spirit. Bliss composes
a "Colour" symphony,

and Liszt records three years of pilgrimage,
including a sonnet

by Petrarch and a "Sonata—after
a lecture of Dante."

Lecture notes, yes; but not a single word.
Brahms, thinking of Schumann,

modulates grief from savage D minors
through enharmonic scales

to major enchantments. Sensualist
and mystic César Franck

chorales wild herds of sound in Sainte Clothilde's.
Percussive consonants

and fluted-vowels played on Proustian lips
(Vinteuill's little phrase)

lisp Ravel's ravishing sevenths and ninths.
Schéhérazade speaking

Russian to dear old Rimsky-Korsakov—
poetry or program

music? Moussorgsky painting his pictures
at an exhibition—

and suppose we mislay the catalogue?
What then? Can we see

by listening? Or hear the sea Wagner,
Debussy and Britten

see and sound so differently? Could we
catch the play of the waves

on Sunday morning or by Moonlight
in a Norwegian fjord

if the words didn't tell us what to see
and hear? Moving in time

but not in space because musical meaning
(unseen noise) is pointless;

43

moving because everything is in
perpetual motion

(see Paganini and Poulenc), well-tempered
transformations of scores

of sequences of signs into folksongs
and dances, melodies

and rhythmic harmonies. "Bookes, songes, ditties
in rime or else in cadence."

Cadential. Deceptive. Worlds without end,
songs without words, sounds

without meaning, memory without...?
Swann's unsingable song,

can you remember how it goes? Is it
Singspiel or *Sprechgesang*?

Elegy

"White Anemones" by William Nicholson:
ghosts of former selves. Carmine and crimson,
coquelicots, poppies of Passchendaele.

Wind-flowers blown open in March or April
—paschal flowers—blown to pieces
through summer and fall, all along the Somme.

Revenants: Osiris, Matthew Shepard, Christ,
warriors known and unknown, flooding memory's defiles
with fragments of life and a fearful desire

for the dead. Generations like leaves: father's fathers,
sons and grandsons—sere, skeletal, gone to earth,
ghosts of ourselves: Nicholson's anemones.

Here, now, in me, seeded by winds of chance,
the men of whom my life is made spring up
Hades-pale to haunt my Pacific dawns,

reproachful because, growing old, I
sometimes forget to water the gardens of Adonis
or wear the flash of blood in my lapel.

45

READING THE SIGNS
(for SH)

1. DO NOT (the sign said)
   DUMP (it plainly read)
   REFUSE. Would you, I asked
   my costive Muse,
   refuse to dump
   if I were death's hostage
   and the ransom
   were a poem not more
   than nine lines long?

2. WATCH OUT
   FOR FALLING ROCKS—
   sky hair other shoes
   blue-chip market prices

   poor Henny
   Penny may
   have mixed up the dates
   or meant the ozone layer.

3. SLIPPERY WHEN WET
   sounds sexy to me
   crossing my bridges
   before I come to them

   YIELD (I must)
   when cruising the trails
   and suddenly alerted to
   SOFT SHOULDERS

46

4. NO WAITING
   even Didi and Gogo
   have turned their backs
   on this suburban black-top

   NO PARKING
   of cars or babies' butts
   no greening
   of America with astroturf

   KEEP OFF THE GRASS
   while play is in progress

   NO SMOKING
   no sniffing
   no mainlining

   NO STOPPING
   him or her, not here
   by woods or any
   where else on on a far
   from frosty evening

   SIGN HERE
   or resign

Man Growing Old

Each day he keeps himself busy, making do
with day-to-day things that have to be done:
the wedding present he once gave; a one-
way ticket for women without a view.
Here he is cooking meals (pasta, stir-fries, stew),
washing underwear and sheets, listing the un-
exceptional jobs that have to be done:
"Replant window-boxes with old-world rue."
He marks time, noting that the trivial round
should furnish all he ought to ask—or so
he hears on Sundays. But, at night, when sound
asleep, and all the common tasks forego
their claims, he dreams of making something new
that can't be made by simply making do.

TWO
POEMS FOR
PHYLLIS WEBB

Another World Crisis

On Friday night, after working late all week on your manuscripts
at the National Library, I dreamed I was in Russia,
in Leningrad, day-dreaming by the frozen canal
or the River Neva, sleet in the wind obscuring the ramp
from the fortress of St Peter and St Paul (tap,tap,tap),
the air thick with thug-talk—*vorovoskoi mir*—rumours
of winter and the black market, soft-sifting, drifting like snow
against the barricades bureaucrats were erecting between me
(with my western mind-set, wandering in uncertain streets:
"This is not Europe you know") and the boxes of documents,
papers published for reasons of national security. Invisible
obstacles stand like ghosts between me and what I thought
I was about to discover, hoped to recover from oblivion,
smuggle out of the building, out of the country. Secret agents,
nationality unknown, insinuate themselves between me
and what I suddenly knew I'd see.

You, there, on the other side
looking down from the fortress, though you couldn't see me
because I was elsewhere, dreaming of you finding a cat here
in St Petersburg, which didn't surprise me, knowing you
receive messages in code from them: Mata Hari sitting between
the colossal paws of Hu, the androsphinx, white sand drifting.
But this cat, this piece of long-haired politics you'd rescued
from the Russian snow, it was Bavarian, you said, a Bavarian
cat. Well, definitely German, anyway.

49

"Make no mistake," you said,
"this cat could not be Russian. I shall take it home with me
and hide it in my basement, the old bomb shelter now filled with junk
and the occasional bottle of Mission Hill, where I live enisled
by salt-stinging seas, several miles south of Amchitka, just north
of Juan de Fuca. And I shall dedicate the rest of my days, already
numbered, from now until November the Fifth, to taking care
of this displaced feline"—none of which surprised me, knowing how crazy
you are—about cats, I mean—how closely you identify with Is'bel
and Leo, Mousekat and Troika, regardless of gender.

"The rest of my life,"
you explain to me in pain, "will turn in two days
one short and one tall. And I'm ordained to collect them all,
to secure them all, make sure these stateless animals have homes."
And truly I wasn't surprised by anything I'd seen or heard,
knowing that in your heart—"in my heart," you said—you knew
the cat was really your brother transformed by your mother
into just another stray: "another world crisis," you exclaimed,
holding up the kitty, "disguising itself in the boxes as a lost Bavarian
Blue"—like me, I thought, sifting through the whispered drafts
of poems, articles and reviews on the banks of the Ottawa River.

50

Returning/Thanks

Floating, like the little lady and the swans in Fulford Harbour, patches of iridescence.
The ferry returning, thanks to wind, wave and motor oil, Phyllis to the mind's Bermudas.

Tidal waters, ceilings, suidical cyclists, red hats, vital organs, gongs. Scattered effects
collapsed into collages. On walls, on window sills, on shelves. All these discomposing matters.

Descending from Maxwell, Erskine, Tuam and Bruce, meaningless messages morse-coded
by mean island spirits: "Are you there? Are you receiving me? Into the bosom of the family?"

A shadow accompanies her, familiar foot-passenger, up the gang-plank. And what a gang!
But she ignores mother, father, brother, lovers, critics devising–I, you, we–strategies.

She is always raising consciousness, for cats, of course, Amnesty International, and words.
She disembarks with the dogs of war leaping around her legs and dreams of the common good

flying about her head. Saint Médard's curse is dissolved for another year, at least. Up in the air,
athwart the wistful sunshine, a pair of hang-gliding poets, wings like unwritten pages.

Here she comes. *Allo! Allo! C'est moi!* She arrives to pick up her car or the mail, local
and international, mainland figure, island woman. Sphinx. A wave. She drives off at once,

disappearing behind her legendary lilac hedge. She shows us nothing for years but we hear
the Wild Woman screaming in her secret garden. Naked, at night, she bathes in Wilson's Bowl.

Postcards from Sri Lanka, index cards from who knows where, litter the floor. Ghazals. Through
the window, water and light. Alone, in the kitchen, she shares her silence with cats we can't see.

51

This first edition of *Untuning the Sky*,
set in Adobe Garamond,
was printed at Black Stone Press (cover)
and Benwell-Atkins (text) for
Pamina Publishing, in July 2000.

The book was designed by David Clifford.